05-Haell

INSIDE THE NFL

BY NICK WELSH
THE CHILD'S WORLD® CHANHASSEN, MINNESOTA

THE DALLAS COWBOYS, THE NEW YORK GIANTS, THE PHILADELPHIA EAGLES, AND THE WASHINGTON REDSKINS

NFC
EAST

INSIDE THE NFL

NFC EAST: The Dallas Cowboys, the New York Giants, the Philadelphia Eagles, and the Washington Redskins

Published in the United States of America by The Child's World®
P.O. Box 326 • Chanhassen, MN 55317-0326 • 800-599-READ • www.childsworld.com

Editorial Directions, Inc.: E. Russell Primm, Editorial Director and Line Editor; Elizabeth K. Martin, Assistant Editor; Olivia Nellums, Editorial Assistant; Susan Hindman, Copy Editor; Susan Ashley, Proofreader; Kevin Cunningham, Fact Checker; Tim Griffin/IndexServ, Indexer; James Buckley Jr., Photo Researcher and Selector

The Child's World®: Mary Berendes, Publishing Director

Photos: All photos Sports Gallery/Al Messerschmidt except AP/Wide World (cover), Corbis (10, 16, 25, 34, 35, 40), Ezra Shaw/Getty Images (1), and Sports Gallery/Cleveland Press (18, 19)

LIBRARY OF CONGRESS CATALOGING-IN-PUBLICATION DATA
Welsh, Nick.
  The NFC East : the Dallas Cowboys, the New York Giants, the Philadelphia Eagles, and the Washington Redskins / by Nick Welsh.
     p. cm. — (The Child's World of sports. Inside the NFL) Includes index.
Summary: Introduces the four teams that form the National Football League's East conference.
  ISBN 1-56766-792-9 (lib. bdg. : alk. paper)
 1. National Football League—History—Juvenile literature. 2. Football—United States—History—Juvenile literature. [1. National Football League—History. 2. Football—History.] I. Title: National Football Conference East. II. Title. III. Series.
  GV955.5.N35W42 2004
  796.332'64'0973—dc21   2003004303

TABLE OF CONTENTS

DALLAS COWBOYS

Year Founded: 1960

Home Stadium: Texas Stadium

Year Stadium Opened: 1971

Team Colors: Silver, blue, and white

The teams playing in the NFC (National Football Conference) East are among the most successful in the history of the NFL (National Football League). They are also among the least successful. The reason for that odd mix is that they're among the very oldest teams of the league. They've had a lot of years to be good—and to be bad!

Three of the four teams—the New York Giants, the Washington Redskins, and the Philadelphia Eagles—have been kicking up dust for more than 70 years. Even the "baby" of the **division**—the Dallas Cowboys—has been breaking hearts and bones for 42 years.

Professional football began in the small towns of the nation's Midwest. However, three of the teams in the NFC East have homes in big cities in the East. Without the crowds of fans in these big cities, pro football might never have become America's most popular sport. Over the years, these four teams have also created some daring new strategies that made the game faster and more fun to watch.

Meanwhile, the athletes playing for these

NEW YORK GIANTS

Year Founded: 1925

Home Stadium: Giants Stadium

Year Stadium Opened: 1976

Team Colors: Blue, white and red

teams—winning or losing—have been among the league's all-time best.

The rivalries between the teams are among the most bitter and exciting in the league. No matter what their records are, for instance, the stakes are always sky-high when the Redskins play the Cowboys. But don't tell that to Philadelphia fans. As far as they're concerned, there's no fiercer rivalry than the one between their team and the Cowboys. Fans of the Giants and Redskins also look forward to all the games between their teams.

One reason NFC East fans might be so intense and dedicated is that their teams have not moved. In fact, since the first of the four teams was founded (the Giants in 1925), only one has moved. And that was all the way back in 1937 when the Redskins moved from Boston to Washington, D.C.

The NFL changed how it is organized in 2002, creating eight divisions of four teams each. However, the league kept these four legendary rivals together. The NFC East remains one of the NFL's most storied and important divisions. Here's the story of nearly a century of ups and downs—but mostly ups.

PHILADELPHIA EAGLES

Year Founded: 1933

Home Stadium: Lincoln Financial Field

Year Stadium Opened: 2003

Team Colors: Green, silver, black and white

WASHINGTON REDSKINS

Year Founded: 1932

Home Stadium: FedEx Field

Year Stadium Opened: 1997

Team Colors: Burgundy and gold

CHAPTER ONE

THE DALLAS COWBOYS

Few teams in NFL history have won so often and so consistently as the Dallas Cowboys. The team set a record with 20 straight winning seasons from 1966 to 1985. But it was not always this way for the Cowboys. When they entered the league in 1960, they lost their first 10 games. The Cowboys didn't win their first game until their second season. And it wasn't until their sixth season in business that the Cowboys managed to even win as many games as they lost.

But the Cowboys' original owner, Clint Murchison Jr., and general manager, Tex Schramm, were very patient. Even as they suffered one losing season after another, they knew they had the key ingredients to build a winning team. The only thing they needed was time.

Head coach Tom Landry had been the defensive genius behind the New York Giants' great teams of the 1950s. Schramm and Murchison were so impressed by Landry's football smarts that they

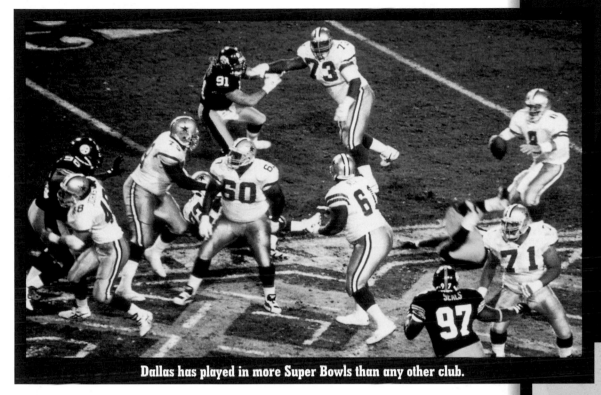

Dallas has played in more Super Bowls than any other club.

signed him for an extra 10 years after his third straight losing season. Gil Brandt was in charge of choosing players. He brought a modern and scientific approach to scouting college players. The first player he ever **drafted** was defensive tackle Bob Lilly, who enjoyed a superb career and was later inducted into the Pro Football Hall of Fame. Schramm himself knew football inside and out. Even more, he understood the importance of television and **marketing,** unlike most owners or

Before playing wide receiver for Dallas from 1965 to 1974, "Bullet" Bob Hayes won the 1964 Olympic gold medal in the 100 meters.

managers of the time. Among his many ideas was television **instant replay**.

The Cowboys have always had great players. But rather than build teams around great players, the Cowboys built their success around a great system. Brandt and Landry had a knack for knowing what players to plug into that system and where. Much sooner than other teams, the Cowboys devised a wide variety of offensive and defensive formations. Just before the ball was snapped, they would shift into

Tom Landry was the Cowboys' coach the first 29 seasons.

another formation to confuse other teams.

On offense, their quarterbacks sometimes lined up a few yards behind the center instead of directly over the center. This **shotgun** formation gives the quarterback a little more time to look downfield for receivers. Roger Staubach combined this strategy with his famous **scrambling** skills to lead Dallas to new heights.

When it came to the Cowboys' defense, size was important. They often drafted very large players — such as Ed "Too Tall"

Roger Staubach was an inspirational leader who had a knack for rallying his team from behind.

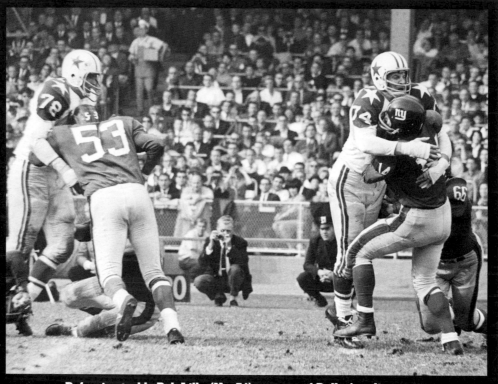

Defensive tackle Bob Lilly (No. 74) was one of Dallas' earliest stars.

Texas Stadium, the Cowboys' home, has a hole in its roof the size of the field. In bad weather, the fans stay dry while the players get wet!

Jones—to stop the run and attack quarterbacks. Under Landry's strict control, the team evolved into an efficient winning machine. He had no patience for those who wouldn't submit to his system. These players, no matter how talented, quickly found themselves traded to other teams.

The Cowboys' patience paid off in the 1971 season when Dallas won Super Bowl VI, its first league championship. Throughout the 1970s, they would

Tony Dorsett once had a 99-yard touchdown run.

Troy Aikman led Dallas to three Super Bowl wins from 1992 to 1995.

remain among the league's best teams. They played in three other Super Bowls that decade, winning Super Bowl XII. The team had some down years in the 1980s until a new owner came into town and cleaned house.

The Cowboys were sold to Jerry Jones in 1989. Legendary coach Landry was fired. Landry's replacement, Jimmy Johnson, suffered two losing years, but he assembled a great core of players. Quarterback Troy Aikman, receiver Michael Irvin, and running back Emmitt Smith made up one of the NFL's best offensive trios.

Aikman was a strong-armed passer with great leadership skills. Irvin combined speed and size to score dozens of touchdowns. Along with Smith, they helped Dallas return to the top of the NFL. The team won three Super Bowls in four seasons, from 1992 to 1995. That brought the Cowboys' total Super Bowl appearances to eight, the most ever. Their five Super Bowl wins are tied with the San Francisco 49ers for most ever.

Smith was the soul of the great Cowboys teams of the 1990s. He led the NFL in rushing four times and set a team record with 1,713 yards in 1992. In

In 1995, Emmitt Smith set an NFL record with 25 touchdowns (a record since broken by Marshall Faulk).

Troy Aikman, Emmitt Smith, and Michael Irvin played together for 10 seasons from 1990 to 1999. They were called the "Triplets."

Emmitt Smith is the NFL's all-time rushing leader.

Bill Parcells, who became the Cowboys' coach in 2003, previously guided the New York Giants and the New England Patriots to the Super Bowl.

1995, he broke his own record by rushing a total of 1,773 yards. Though smaller than some runners, he was a determined, powerful player. On his way to becoming the NFL's all-time leading rusher in 2002, Smith made millions of fans.

The Cowboys continue to be one of the most popular NFL teams, if not among the most successful recently. But with a case full of trophies to inspire them, maybe today's Cowboys can make one more ride at the NFL title.

CHAPTER TWO

THE NEW YORK GIANTS

The Giants were formed in 1925, when Tim Mara, a professional gambler, bought the team rights for $500. Because the team is worth more than $300 million today, you might say that was a good investment. Mara named the team after New York's baseball team, which also played in the Polo Grounds. At that time, professional football was not nearly as popular as it is today. Within months, Mara had lost $40,000 on his new ball club. He might have gone out of business. However, a super player named Red Grange attracted 70,000 people to see him play against the Giants. Mara's team was saved.

In 1927, the Giants won more games than any other team and held opponents to a season total of only 20 points. In 1930, Tim Mara gave the team to his two sons, Jack and Wellington. At that time, Wellington Mara was only 14 years old, making him the youngest person to ever own a football team. More than 70 years later, Wellington Mara still

Steve Owen coached the Giants for 23 seasons.

owns half of the team and is seen regularly at team practices and games.

In 1931, the Giants hired Steve Owen as coach. Owen had been a stellar tackle for the Giants, and he would end up being coach for 23 years. Under

Owen, the Giants played in the very first NFL Championship Game against the Chicago Bears in 1933. However, the Bears beat the Giants 23–21 in a classic nail-biter where the lead changed no less than six times.

The next year, 1934, the Giants made it to the championship, again facing the Bears. On game day, the temperature was nine degrees and the ground was hard as ice. None of the players could get traction with their cleats. At halftime, the Giants' trainer gave his players "basketball shoes"—sneakers. This gave the Giants a huge advantage over the Bears. They scored four touchdowns in the second half to win. The contest is still remembered as "The Sneakers Game."

Under Owen, the Giants remained contenders until the end of World War II. He was replaced in 1954 by Jim Lee Howell, an ex-Marine and also a former Giant. Between 1956 and 1963, the Giants placed first in their division six times over the next eight seasons. They won the NFL championship in 1956 and played in the championship games of 1958 and 1959, losing both to the Colts. (The 1958 game is still called "The Greatest Game Ever

Giants end Red Badgro scored the very first touchdown ever in an NFL Championship Game, in the 1933 loss to Chicago.

Mindful of the 1934 title game, the Giants came out in sneakers at the start of the 1956 title game and routed Chicago 47–7 on an icy field.

Sam Huff was a Hall of Fame linebacker for the Giants.

Played." Giants fans might not think so, but the Colts' thrilling **overtime** win remains a classic.)

The Giants had an abundance of talent: quarterbacks Charlie Connerly and Y. A. Tittle, running back Frank Gifford, linebacker Sam Huff, and defensive back Emlen Tunnell, to name just a few. Two assistant coaches, Vince Lombardi and Tom Landry, later became legendary head coaches.

However, after 1963, the Giants experienced a 20-year downhill slide. They

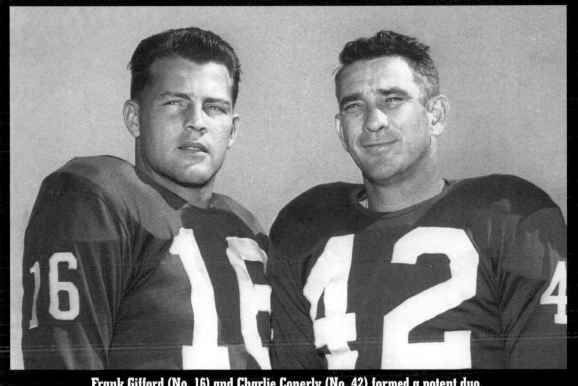

Frank Gifford (No. 16) and Charlie Conerly (No. 42) formed a potent duo.

would play in four different "home" stadiums. They finally moved into Giants Stadium in New Jersey in 1976. However, they finished last or next-to-last eight times between 1976 and 1987.

But in the 1980s, under coach Bill Parcells, the Giants transformed themselves. They turned from the 98-pound (44.5-kilogram) weakling of the league to the 900-pound (409-kg) gorilla. Offensively, the Giants' game plan was simple,

During the 1930s and 1940s, Giants tough-guy Mel Hein played both offense and defense and didn't miss a game for 15 years!

Lawrence Taylor was the dominant defensive player of the 1980s.

Phil Simms is the Giants' all-time leading passer.

basic, and aggressive. They focused heavily on running the ball. On defense, they were fierce. Linebacker Lawrence Taylor was the best ever to play the position. When he was in the game, it felt as though the Giants had 15 men on the field. Other teams often **double-teamed** Taylor (or triple-teamed him!), which freed up his teammates to make the play. But Taylor still was the most dominant player. Taylor and Parcells led the Giants to victories in Super Bowls XXI and XXV.

The 1986 Giants popularized the now-widespread tradition of dousing the head coach with ice water or a sports drink after a big victory.

In 1991, Wellington Mara sold half of the team
to Robert Tisch. The Mara family had been the sole
owners of the Giants for 66 years. The Giants are
no longer the family business they used to be, but
they still are winners.

In 2000, the Giants looked like heroes of the
past. With five games to play, Coach Jim Fassel
stunned the media, not to mention his players. He
announced that the team wouldn't lose any more

Michael Strahan set an NFL record with 22.5 sacks in 2001.

Tiki Barber ran for a career-best 1,387 yards in 2002.

games. Amazingly, they did what their coach said. They won their last five games and then a trip to Super Bowl XXXV. However, like Giants teams of the past, they lost to a team from Baltimore. Though it was the Ravens this time and not the Colts, it seemed sadly familiar.

THE PHILADELPHIA EAGLES

In 1933, Bert Bell and Lud Wray bought an NFL franchise for Philadelphia. They named the team the Eagles after the symbol of the New Deal's National Recovery Administration. But the Eagles needed more than a name to fly. In their opening game, they lost 56–0. In 1936, they lost 11 straight games, including six without scoring. It would be 11 years before they had a winning record.

Under coach Earl "Greasy" Neale, who took over in 1941, the Eagles became a top team. Hard-charging running back Steve Van Buren led the attack, while end Pete Pihos was one of the league's best. As good as the Eagles' offense was, it was the defense that opponents most feared. In 1948 and 1949, the Eagles won the NFL title. In both championship games, they shut out their opponents (the Chicago Cardinals and the Los Angeles Rams). No other team since has done this.

In the 1948 championship game, a blinding

snowstorm made the field nearly invisible. Players huddled under straw blankets on the sidelines. Amid the tough conditions, the Eagles' defense limited the Cardinals to just six first downs. Van Buren scored the game's only points on a 5-yard touchdown run. Bad weather dominated the following year's championship, too. Heavy rains transformed the field into a muddy river. However, Van Buren

In 1943, with many players serving in the military, the Eagles combined with the Pittsburgh Steelers. The combined team was 5–4–1 and called the Steagles.

Steve Van Buren was the star of the 1948 and 1949 champions.

The Eagles selected back Jay Berwanger with the first pick in the first NFL draft in 1936, but the Heisman Trophy winner never played pro football.

splashed through the puddles to run for a then-record 196 yards.

That 1949 team included Chuck Bednarik, one of the toughest and most punishing players ever to lace up football cleats. As a linebacker and center, he was one of the last players to play both offense and defense. "Concrete Charley" played in 253 out

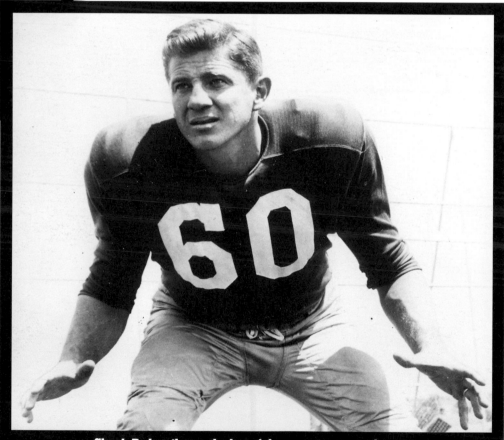

Chuck Bednarik was the last of the great two-way players.

of a possible 256 games during his 14-year career. During the 1960 championship game won by Philadelphia, Bednarik played all but two of the 60 minutes On the last play of the game, he saved the win by stopping Green Bay fullback Jim Taylor from scoring. Leading the Eagles offense in that game was Hall of Fame quarterback Norm Van Brocklin.

In the 1960 title game, the Eagles handed Packers coach Vince Lombardi the only postseason defeat of his legendary career.

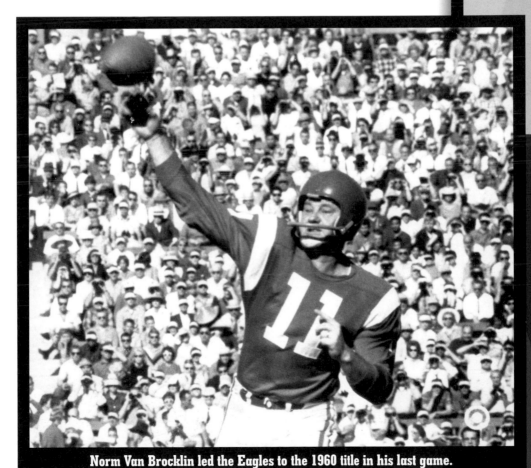

Norm Van Brocklin led the Eagles to the 1960 title in his last game.

Ron Jaworski's nickname is Jaws. He has become a popular football commentator on ESPN.

Coach Dick Vermeil retired to the broadcast booth in 1982. He came out of retirement in 1997 and led the Rams to the Super Bowl two seasons later.

After winning the 1960 championship—and coming close the next year—the Eagles slid steadily downhill for nearly 20 years. By the early 1970s, the Eagles were not just losing, but fighting among themselves. One coach called the team's owner "a man of little character," and was fired. After he was fired, his replacement—who believed in a military-style of team discipline—ordered all players to cut their hair short and shave their beards and mustaches. None of this produced a winning season.

Things changed for the better in 1976 when the Eagles hired Dick Vermeil as head coach. Strict, hard working, and emotional, Vermeil pushed his players to new levels. Quarterback Ron Jaworski was smart, sturdy, and dependable. Wide receiver Harold Carmichael was 6 feet 8 inches (203 centimeters) tall, and still holds the Eagles record for receptions. Ferocious linebacker Bill Bergey led the defense. Running back Wilbert Montgomery became the team's all-time leader in rushing yards. The revamped Eagles made it to the playoffs four years in a row from 1978 to 1981. In 1980, they reached Super Bowl XV, losing to the Oakland Raiders.

Harold Carmichael is the Eagles' all-time leading receiver.

Reggie White's specialty was sacking the quarterback.

Randall Cunningham made big plays passing and running.

Defensive genius Buddy Ryan took over as coach in 1986. With the Eagles, Ryan created a defensive machine that scared opponents before they stepped foot on the field. Defensive linemen Reggie White and Jerome Brown shut down opponents' running games and ate quarterbacks for lunch. Quarterback Randall Cunningham was a gifted long passer and a great scrambler, but he was inconsistent. The Eagles made the playoffs four times between 1988 and 1992, but never advanced past the divisional round.

The Eagles moved into a brand-new stadium in 2003, built in the parking lot of their former home, Veterans Stadium.

Current coach Andy Reid has rallied the Eagles back to winning form. Quarterback Donovan McNabb is 6 foot, 2 inches (188 cm), 226 pounds (103 kg), and as big, fast, and strong as many of the players trying to tackle him. Reid also coaches the traditional run-crushing Eagles defense.

Though they are used to heartbreak and disappointment, Eagles fans are still hopeful. Famous for being quick to boo their team, they're also always ready to cheer a winner.

Though he didn't realize it, Donovan McNabb broke his ankle early in a game against Arizona in 2002. He still passed for 4 touchdowns and led the Eagles to a win.

Donovan McNabb has helped make the Eagles winners again.

CHAPTER FOUR

THE WASHINGTON REDSKINS

When owner George Preston Marshall of Boston first entered the NFL in 1932, he called the team the Braves. He chose that name because his club played on the same field as the Boston Braves baseball team. He changed the name to Redskins in 1933. Playing off the team's new name, he had his players show up for team photographs dressed in war paint and war bonnets. He even hired a Native American, William "Lone Star" Dietz, to coach the team.

(At the time, no one objected to the team's new name. However, these days, many Native Americans object to the name. They feel that the word is a racist slur. However, the team says that it honors the brave and powerful Native American warriors. In any case, the games—and the controversy—go on.)

The early Boston teams starred running back Cliff Battles. He was the first player ever to rush for more than 200 yards in a game. But the team as a whole played poorly. In 1937, Marshall moved

In the late 1930s,
Redskins coach
Ray Flaherty
introduced the
screen pass.
Now a regular part
of the NFL, it helped
Washington win
its first title.

the team to Washington, D.C. The team's new hometown was rewarded with the Redskins' first NFL championship. They were led by **rookie** quarterback "Slingin'" Sammy Baugh.

During his 16-year career, Baugh—a tough, rawboned quarterback out of Texas—set dozens of records. At that time, players were expected to play both offense and defense. In a 1943 game against the Detroit Lions, Baugh threw four touchdown passes and also intercepted four passes. That year,

The Redskins won the 1937 title their first year in Washington.

Sammy Baugh (33) was a star on offense, defense and special teams.

he led the league in punting, passing, and interceptions—an accomplishment that will never be equaled. His career average of 45.1 yards per punt remains an all-time record.

Far more than most team owners, Marshall understood football was as much a spectacle as it was a sport. In 1937, he arranged a parade of 10,000 Washington fans up Broadway in New York City behind the Redskins' marching band. Marshall introduced the marching band to football, as well as the team song and the halftime show. It was also his idea to split the league's teams into two divisions

The words to the Redskins' fight song were co-written by George Preston Marshall's wife, Corinne Griffith, who was a silent-film star.

and have the winners of each play for the championship. Before that, the team with the best record was declared champion. Marshall understood the passing game was more thrilling to fans. He helped have the football itself redesigned to make it easier to throw. He originated the idea of the Pro Bowl game, the league's annual all-star game.

Marshall was also famously cheap. He personally chased after footballs kicked or thrown into the stands, retrieving them from unhappy fans. At first, he decided to do without team **scouts.** He chose instead to draft college players based on what he'd read in a few sports magazines. Much of what he did worked, and the Redskins were among the league leaders. They hit a bump in the road in 1940, however. They lost the NFL Championship Game to the Chicago Bears 73–0. It remains the most lopsided game in league history and the record for most points scored.

Between 1946 and 1969, the Redskins ranked as one of the worst teams in football. In that time, they won more than half their games in only three seasons. Part of the problem was that Marshall had been reluctant to hire African-American players.

Bobby Mitchell helped integrate the Redskins—
and make them winners.

Quarterback Sonny Jurgensen had a powerful right arm.

When Bobby Mitchell finally joined the team in 1962, it helped the team improve. Quarterback Sonny Jurgensen, one of the greatest pure passers of all time, also joined the team. Jurgensen teamed up with Mitchell and fellow receiver Charley Taylor to lead the 'Skins to some good seasons.

In 1971, Coach George Allen took over and began to rally the team. In his rush to victory, Allen traded away many talented young players for seasoned veterans. His teams were known as the Over-the-Hill Gang. Allen's team made it to Super Bowl VII in 1972 and never had a losing season.

The Redskins rode John Riggins to the NFL title in 1982.

Beginning in 1981, with the hiring of Joe Gibbs as coach, the Redskins achieved their greatest glory. During Gibbs's 12 years, the Redskins went to the Super Bowl four times and won three. The real stars of Gibbs's teams were not flashy quarterbacks but sturdy offensive linemen, nicknamed the "Hogs." The Hogs ripped open huge holes for punishing running backs like John Riggins. The Hogs were so popular that a group of Redskins fans started showing up to games dressed as "Hogettes."

In his 11 seasons as coach, Joe Gibbs led the Redskins to three Super Bowl victories—with three different starting quarterbacks.

39

Steve Spurrier was a successful college coach before joining Washington.

After leaving the NFL in 1992, Joe Gibbs turned to owning a NASCAR team. His racers have won two Winston Cup titles, including Tony Stewart in 2002.

They wore women's clothes and had plastic pig snouts strapped to their faces.

Since Gibbs's departure, the Redskins' fortunes have been up and down. In 1994, they lost 13 games. In 1997, they moved from their previous home in RFK Stadium to their present location at FedEx Field. A big change came in 1999 when young Daniel Snyder bought the team. He spent a lot of money and made a lot of headlines, but has not turned his team into a winner yet. He hired a big-name coach, Steve Spurrier, in 2002, but had trouble getting top players.

In the worst of times and the best of times, few

fans are as loyal to their team as Redskins' fans. The waiting list for season tickets is decades long. In 2000, though the team finished only 8–8, it set an all-time attendance record.

That's one thing that all the teams of the NFC East have in common. Their loyal fans stick with them through thick and thin. However, with every team having a championship in its past, those fans are hoping for history to repeat itself—sooner rather than later!

The Redskins didn't tell rookie Timmy Smith he was starting Super Bowl XXII until the day of the game. He went on to run for a record 204 yards.

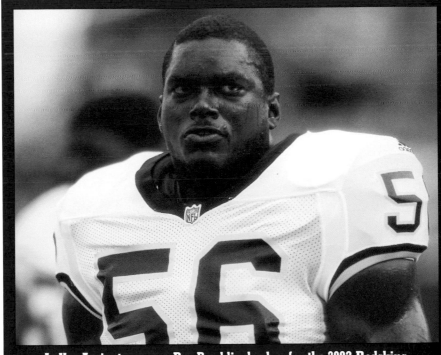

LaVar Arrington was a Pro Bowl linebacker for the 2002 Redskins.

STAT STUFF

TEAM RECORDS

Team	All-time Record	NFL Titles (Most Recent)	Number of Times in Playoffs	Top Coach (Wins)
DALLAS	357–269–6	5 (1995)	26	Tom Landry (270)
NEW YORK	567–465–33	5 (1990)	26	Steve Owen (153)
PHILADELPHIA	424–489–24	3 (1960)	17	Greasy Neale (66)
WASHINGTON	495–440–27	7 (1991)	20	Joe Gibbs (140)

MEMBERS OF THE PRO FOOTBALL HALL OF FAME

DALLAS

Player	Position	Date Inducted
Herb Adderley	Cornerback	1980
Lance Alworth	Flanker	1978
Mike Ditka	Tight End	1988
Tony Dorsett	Running Back	1994
Forrest Gregg	Tackle/Guard	1977
Tom Landry	Coach	1990
Bob Lilly	Defensive Tackle	1980
Tommy McDonald	Wide Receiver	1998
Mel Renfro	Cornerback/Safety	1996
Texas E. (Tex) Schramm	Administrator	1991
Jackie Smith	Tight End	1994
Roger Staubach	Quarterback	1985
Randy White	Defensive Tackle	1994

PHILADELPHIA

Player	Position	Date Inducted
Chuck Bednarik	Center/Linebacker	1967
Bert Bell	Owner/Administrator	1963
Mike Ditka	Tight End	1988
Bill Hewitt	End	1971
Sonny Jurgensen	Quarterback	1983
Ollie Matson	Halfback	1972
Tommy McDonald	Wide Receiver	1998
Earle (Greasy) Neale	Coach	1969
Pete Pihos	End	1970
Jim Ringo	Center	1981
Norm Van Brocklin	Quarterback	1971
Steve Van Buren	Halfback	1965
Alex Wojciechowicz	Center/Linebacker	1968

NEW YORK

Player	Position	Date Inducted
Red Badgro	End	1981
Roosevelt Brown	Offensive Tackle	1975
Larry Csonka	Fullback	1987
Ray Flaherty	Coach	1976
Frank Gifford	Halfback/Flanker	1977
Joe Guyon	Halfback	1966
Mel Hein	Center	1963
Wilbur (Pete) Henry	Tackle	1963
Arnie Herber	Quarterback	1966
Robert (Cal) Hubbard	Tackle	1963
Sam Huff	Linebacker	1982
Alphonse (Tuffy) Leemans	Halfback/Fullback	1978
Tim Mara	Administrator	1963
Wellington Mara	Owner/Administrator	1997
Don Maynard	Wide Receiver	1987
Hugh McElhenny	Halfback	1970
Steve Owen	Coach/Tackle	1966
Andy Robustelli	Defensive End	1971
Ken Strong	Halfback	1967
Fran Tarkenton	Quarterback	1986
Lawrence Taylor	Linebacker	1999
Jim Thorpe	Halfback	1963
Y. A. Tittle	Quarterback	1971
Emlen Tunnell	Defensive Back	1967
Arnie Weinmeister	Defensive Tackle	1984

WASHINGTON

Player	Position	Date Inducted
George Allen	Coach	2002
Cliff Battles	Halfback	1968
Sammy Baugh	Quarterback	1963
Bill Dudley	Halfback	1966
Albert Glen (Turk) Edwards	Tackle	1969
Ray Flaherty	Coach	1976
Joe Gibbs	Coach	1996
Ken Houston	Strong Safety	1986
Sam Huff	Linebacker	1982
David (Deacon) Jones	Defensive End	1980
Stan Jones	Guard/Defensive Tackle	1991
Sonny Jurgensen	Quarterback	1983
Paul Krause	Safety	1998
Earl (Curly) Lambeau	Coach	1963
Vince Lombardi	Coach	1971
George Preston Marshall	Administrator	1963
Wayne Millner	End	1968
Bobby Mitchell	Wide Receiver/Halfback	1983
John Riggins	Running Back	1992
Charley Taylor	Wide Receiver	1984

STAT STUFF

NFC EAST CAREER LEADERS (THROUGH 2002)

DALLAS

Category	Name (Years with Team)	Total
Rushing	Emmitt Smith (1990–2002)	17,162
Passing yards	Troy Aikman (1989–2000)	32,942
Touchdown passes	Troy Aikman (1989–2000)	165
Receptions	Michael Irvin (1988–1999)	750
Touchdowns	Emmitt Smith (1990–2002)	164
Scoring	Emmitt Smith (1990–2002)	986

PHILADELPHIA

Category	Name (Years with Team)	Total
Rushing	Wilbert Montgomery (1977–1984)	6,538
Passing yards	Ron Jaworski (1977–1986)	26,963
Touchdown passes	Ron Jaworski (1977–1986)	175
Receptions	Harold Carmichael (1971–1983)	589
Touchdowns	Harold Carmichael (1971–1983)	79
Scoring	Bobby Walston (1951–1962)	881

NEW YORK

Category	Name (Years with Team)	Total
Rushing	Rodney Hampton (1990–97)	6,897
Passing yards	Phil Simms (1979–1993)	33,462
Touchdown passes	Phil Simms (1979–1993)	199
Receptions	Joe Morrison (1959–1972)	395
Touchdowns	Frank Gifford (1952–1964)	78
Scoring	Pete Gogolak (1966–1974)	646

WASHINGTON

Category	Name (Years with Team)	Total
Rushing	John Riggins (1976–79, 1981–85)	7,472
Passing yards	Joe Theismann (1974–1985)	25,206
Touchdown passes	Sammy Baugh (1937–1952)	187
Receptions	Art Monk (1980–1993)	888
Touchdowns	Charley Taylor (1964–1977)	90
Scoring	Mark Moseley (1974–1986)	1,206

GLOSSARY

divisions—in the NFL, teams are placed in one of these four-team groups

double-teamed—defended or blocked by more than one player

drafting—the process of adding new players to an NFL team by selecting college players in the annual draft

instant replay—when a TV network shows a play again, right after it has been aired live

marketing—the use of advertising and other activities to get someone to buy or attend something

overtime—a period of play after the regular time; played if the score is tied after regulation

rookie—a player in his first season in pro sports

scouts—football experts hired by teams to look for college players to draft or to look ahead at future opponents

scrambling—when a quarterback runs, whether to buy time to find a receiver or to run downfield to gain yards

screen pass—a short pass thrown to a player behind the line of scrimmage; blockers then move in front of the receiver as a screen to help him move downfield

shotgun—the name of a formation in which the quarterback receives the snap several yards behind the line of scrimmage

TIME LINE

1925 New York Giants founded; they join five-year-old NFL

1932 Washington Redskins founded as Boston Braves

1934 Giants win NFL championship

1938 Giants win NFL championship

1942 Redskins win NFL championship

1948 Eagles win the first of two straight NFL titles.

1956 Giants win NFL championship

1960 Dallas Cowboys founded as expansion team; Philadelphia wins NFL title

1971 Dallas wins Super Bowl VI

1977 Dallas wins Super Bowl XII

1982 Washington wins Super Bowl XVII

1986 Giants win Super Bowl XXI

1987 Washington wins Super Bowl XXII

1991 Giants win Super Bowl XXV

1992 Washington wins Super Bowl XXVI

1996 Dallas wins Super Bowl XXX, its third Super Bowl win in four seasons

FOR MORE INFORMATION ABOUT THE NFC EAST AND THE NFL

BOOKS

Buckley, James Jr. *Rumbling Running Backs*. New York: DK Publishing, 2001.

Buckley, James Jr., and Jerry Rice. *America's Greatest Game*. New York: Hyperion Books for Children, 1998.

Grabowski, John. *The Dallas Cowboys*. San Diego: Lucent Books, 2001.

Whittingham, Richard. *Hail Redskins*. Chicago: Triumph Books, 2001.

ON THE WEB

Visit our home page for lots of links about the NFC East:
http://www.childsworld.com/links.html
Note to Parents, Teachers, and Librarians: We routinely verify our Web links to make sure they are safe, active sites—so encourage your readers to check them out!

INDEX

ABOUT THE AUTHOR

Nick Welsh is an award-winning writer for the *Santa Barbara Independent* weekly. He is also a lifelong football fan and "weekend warrior" touch-football player. He has contributed to other major newspapers and magazines in California and nationwide. This is his first book for young readers.